Worldwide Opportunities in Travel and Tourism

By

Adam Starchild

Books for Business
New York - Hong Kong

Worldwide Opportunities in Travel and Tourism

by
Adam Starchild

ISBN: 0-89499-235-X

Books for Business
New York - Hong Kong
http://www.BusinessBooksInternational.com

Contents

Introduction

During the last quarter of the 20th century, the travel and tourism industry has developed into one of the fastest growing sectors of the global economy. More people than ever travel for business and pleasure to destinations around the world. In the U.S., travel and tourism account for close to 7% of the GNP, making it the second largest sector of the country's economy. In 1999, U.S. travel agencies sold close to $50 billion worth of tickets and billions more in travel-related services. As impressive as these numbers are, they are only a part of the travel services sold throughout the world.

Travel and tourism have clearly become big business. There are many reasons for this. Competition among international and regional airlines has made air travel accessible and affordable for people everywhere. Many countries – particularly those of the former Communist bloc – that once discouraged visitors have opened their borders and now welcome tourists and the money they bring. The population of the U.S., as well as Asia and Japan, is graying. Many of these individuals are at the peak of their earning

1

years, their children are grown or nearly grown, and they enjoy much discretionary income. While they may not consider themselves wealthy, they can afford to travel, which they do regularly. Moreover, there is a significant and growing "retired" population in many Western countries that enjoys traveling. These factors virtually ensure continued growth for the travel and tourism industry, both in the U.S. and throughout the world.

The travel and tourism industry is broad and diversified. In its narrowest definition, it includes those enterprises directly related to travel – airlines, cruise lines, travel agents, hotels, car rental companies, and tours. At its broadest, it includes any business that concentrates the bulk of its operation on travel- or tourist-related activities. These might include restaurants, night clubs, gift shops, amusement and theme parks, campgrounds, marketing firms that specialize in travel and tourism, and special activities such as horseback riding, white-water rafting, and skiing. Of course, these are just some examples, and creative entrepreneurs can undoubtedly find countless niche businesses that can provide special products or services to travelers and vacationers.

Entrepreneurs will undoubtedly find numerous opportunities in the industry. Indeed, it is not so difficult finding an opportunity, but rather choosing the best one, an enterprise that is personally satisfying and which has a superior chance for success and profitability.

While many large businesses account for millions of travel and tourism dollars, the industry has plenty of room for small operations. It has, in fact, been estimated that up to 99% of the U.S. businesses whose major activity is travel and tourism are considered to be small by federal standards. Herein lies the great opportunities for entrepreneurs.

Many businesses whose services and products that target tourists and travelers can be started for minimal investments. This is especially true in many countries whose governments encourage investment in an effort to stimulate local economies and expand the travel and tourism industry within their borders. Many nations foster economic development and investment through a variety of incentives, including reduced tax rates, tax holidays, or special grants to underwrite the cost of facilities or train local workers. Such incentives can greatly enhance an operation's overall profitability.

Because much of the United States is saturated with businesses that serve the needs of travelers, the greatest opportunities for entrepreneurs in the travel and tourism sector are found in other lands. While travel and tourism companies abound in places like the Bahamas, Bermuda, and the Cayman

Islands, there are numerous other sites where the opportunities are boundless. As the global economy expands, many of these places are on the verge of becoming major tourist and travel sites, but they have not achieved that status yet. There is plenty of opportunity for enterprising individuals to start and build companies. The key is to identify these sites and establish a business before the competition arrives.

This, obviously, can be difficult when considering foreign sites located around the world. It is essential that you personally visit any place in which you are considering investing. Selecting possible investment sites from brochures, videos provided by embassies, or tips from friends or colleagues is one of the surest ways to secure failure and nothing else.

So how does one manage to visit potential sites that may be found in Europe, the Middle East, Asia, Africa, or South America without incurring burdensome travel costs? You might, for example, plan your vacation to the Nevis, the Azores, or Seychelles and use some of your time there to scout potential tourism investments. In this way you are combining pleasure and business and may even be able to deduct some of the expenses from your taxes. This is not the most efficient method, though. By far the best is to use your enthusiasm for entrepreneurship and establish a home-based travel agency.

Once you establish a travel agency you will gain numerous advantages. Along with being able to deduct business expenses which can reduce your tax burden, you will be able to take advantage of familiarization tours offered by travel-service providers. Such tours, usually offered at deep discounts, will give you the opportunity to visit various places around the world, where you can evaluate potential investments. Not only will you have the chance to see the area and mingle with its people, you will be able to assess the business climate and potential for investment.

You can benefit from establishing a travel agency even if you limit the scope of your agency. Most home-based travel agents work with host agencies, larger agencies which provide tickets and in many cases manage the bookings for lodging. The home-based travel agent's primary task is to provide clients for the host agency. Nonetheless, the home-based agent enjoys all of the advantages of being a travel agent. For the entrepreneur who seeks to build a travel/tourism business, establishing a travel agency is the first step to worldwide investment.

The usual cautions, of course, apply. Although opportunities in travel and tourism may be found the world over, creating a successful business requires good business sense, an understanding of how to properly build a company, and hard work. For those entrepreneurs capable of satisfying these demands, the returns are truly great. Few enterprises are as challenging, exciting, and rewarding as creating a business in an area in which the potential for growth is exceptional and one's success is entirely dependent upon his or her knowledge and business skills. The travel and tourism sector offers such opportunity in locations around the world.

Over the past several years, travel and tourism have constituted one of the fastest growing sectors in the world economy. For much of the past three decades, annual growth has averaged 10% or more, with several countries averaging significantly more. This trend is expected to continue, fueled by increasing numbers of people who travel for pleasure and business.

Worldwide Opportunities in Travel and Tourism

As the travel and tourism industry expands, reaching into more and more parts of the world that not long ago were either closed to visitors or did not have much to offer, the opportunities for establishing successful businesses in the sector increase. A few examples illustrate this point well.

- Thirty years ago Costa Rica for much of the world's travelers was a destination of little interest. Today it is a retirement haven for Americans as well as a prime vacation spot known for the natural beauty of its landscape and biodiversity of its lush forests.

- Not long ago, African safaris were an activity reserved for the adventurous and well-to-do. Today ordinary families desiring a vacation different from the typical fare offered at resorts consider safaris to be delightful alternatives.

- Within the last twenty years cruise lines have expanded their routes and regularly visit ports throughout the Caribbean, Mediterranean, Eastern Pacific, and Alaska.

- Big resorts and theme parks have been built throughout the world during the last few decades and attract millions of visitors every year.

- Whereas a European vacation was thought to be out of the reach of most Americans 25 years ago, European tours are filled with Americans today.

- During the last quarter of the century affordable air fare has made the world smaller, and now allows people to visit places that would have been too costly in the past. In many cases, only big cities were served by airlines, but today regional and family-run airlines provide service to the most distant places.

- It was not too many years ago that people brought airline tickets only when they had to travel great distances – for business or for vacation. Now, many people fly frequently, not only for business and vacation travel but as a method of commuting. Consider that holidays such as Thanksgiving and Christmas are some of the busiest days at airports as people return home for the holidays. Certainly they can drive home, but flying is far faster and efficient.

- As the new century begins, Americans, Europeans, and Asians are traveling more than ever to more places than ever.

These are just some examples of the steady growth of the travel and tourism industry over the past few decades. When most people think of the travel and tourism industry, they think of airlines, resorts, tours, and cruise lines. Typically, these are provided by major corporations. Most people don't realize that most businesses in the travel and tourism sector are small. Most are family owned and a large percentage have carved out niche markets.

The travel and tourism industry is comprised of millions of companies worldwide, including:

- Major providers: airlines, cruise lines, resorts, hotels, motels, bed and breakfast inns, tour operators, buslines, and restaurants.

- Rental companies offering: cars, bicycles, boats, special equipment such as rafts (for white-water rafting), skis, snowboards, etc.

- Theme and amusement parks.

- Providers of special activities: tours, hiking trails, nature walks, horseback riding, scuba diving, etc.

9

- Night clubs and lounges.

- Stores and shops selling: food, gifts, hunting and fishing equipment, boats and boating equipment, antiques, and local specialties.

- Campgrounds.

- Providers of handicrafts.

- Providers of local foods: bakeries, fisherman, farmers, etc.

- Providers of guides, information services, etc.

- Taxi companies.

- Sports facilities.

- Theaters.

- Manufacturers of equipment for travel and tourism, including recreational items.

- Travel agencies.

- Marketing companies that provide services to companies involved in travel and tourism.

- Publishers of travel brochures, maps, information booklets.

- Service companies that support travel and tourism: maintenance firms, janitorial companies, landscaping firms, etc.

When one considers the scope of companies the above list includes, it is clear that entrepreneurs have numerous choices of enterprises. It becomes incumbent upon the entrepreneur to identify a business he enjoys and establish it in a location where it is most likely to prosper. This requires careful evaluation of the business climate and potential market of possible sites.

Opportunities in Emerging Economies

While opening a successful travel-related business in New York City may be an admirable goal, it is likely to be difficult to achieve a high level of profitability because the New York market is saturated with travel companies. Unless you truly find and develop a niche – a special market that you can exploit more efficiently than your competitors – building your business will be extremely hard. This will be the case in any city or region where travel and tourism companies are plentiful.

With the worldwide growth of the industry, however, travel business opportunities may be found today in places they did not exist as short as a year ago. The industry is growing rapidly and new opportunities are developing every day.

While these opportunities may be found in countries the world over, by far the best opportunities are developing in emerging economies. It is critical that the entrepreneur consider the entire world as a place for possible investment with his focus on areas that are experiencing rapid growth. Many of the most successful entrepreneurs today are those who consider themselves global entrepreneurs.

Individuals who limit themselves to investments within their native lands severely undermine their chances to find exceptional opportunities. Without question, some of the best opportunities for investment in the current economic climate are overseas. Novice entrepreneurs are often unsure how to begin an effective search for investment opportunities in other countries, but there are, in fact, several steps that can help you identify potential sites for the creation of a travel and tourism company.

Identifying the best sites and opportunities requires thoughtful research and assessment. The first step is to become a student of the world economic scene. Watch business news reports, subscribe to and study economic journals, and research the economic and political environment of countries with developing economies. Contact the embassies of countries in which you are interested and request information packets regarding investment. Selecting nations with bright economic futures and which encourage foreign investment is critical, for it will be these lands that offer the greatest promise of high returns on your investment. Be cautious of sites containing established travel/tourism companies, because the competition there will be high and it will be difficult to build a new business.

After identifying potential sites for the establishment of a business, you must consider which type of business to start. While this may not be a firm decision at this point – you may find later that a different type of business will likely enjoy more profitability at this place – you should have a general idea of what you would like to do. This will help to guide you in your continued research efforts. Perhaps you will consider a company that provides tours for people who wish to see interior mountains, or you might find that a prime tourist site in a particular locale would benefit from a new restaurant, or you might find a market for the manufacturer of local products that can be sold as souvenirs. You should consider only businesses in which you have a high degree of interest, because that interest will provide you with the motivation to see your business succeed.

Once you have identified a site and decided on the kind of business you would like to establish, you must visit the site in which you are considering investing to evaluate the viability of your enterprise. There is much you must assess, including:

- The site's political climate. Does the government foster foreign investment? How welcome would you be? Many emerging nations encourage international investment as a means of fueling their economies. You must also determine how stable the country is. Countries in which the government is weak or there is significant political unrest are often poor choices for investment.

- The site's laws. Most North Americans and many Western Europeans are most comfortable in lands where the laws are based on English common law and democracy is practiced.

- The site's business climate. Does the government support a pro-business environment through legislation and practice? Some government's offer a wide variety of incentives for investors, including substantial tax breaks, reduced tariffs on imported equipment, liaison agencies that promote investment and reduce red tape, and government grants that may be applied to facilities and the training of a workforce.

• The site's people. Are they educated? In many nations with emerging economies, a sizable percentage of the population may be poorly educated, but there is a significant number that is. These people will comprise the foundation of the nation's economy. If they are in short supply, economic growth will falter. Another point of concern is language. In many places English is the language of business but not everywhere. If you do not speak the common language of the country in which you are considering investing, and if the populace does not speak English, you will be at a serious disadvantage. Yet another concern is whether you will be able to hire people from the local workforce to manage your business. Even if you intend to work in your company, you will need workers and it is most practical to hire them from the local population.

• The site's social structure. Will the people of the country accept your presence. Although many sites welcome investment because of the jobs new companies create and the boost they provide to local economies, there still are some places in which foreigners are not welcome, despite government support. Never ignore the sentiments of the residents. Good relations with townspeople and local leaders will do much to nurture the growth of your business.

- Before making any verbal commitments or signing any agreements or contracts, check with your attorney. Have him review all documents meticulously. You should select attorneys who have experience with international business practices. If he feels that anything is out of order, carefully reconsider your situation before continuing.

When you visit a site, always mingle with the general population. Some countries maintain agencies whose purpose is to promote foreign investment. While these individuals can streamline the way to the establishment of a business, in their zeal to encourage foreign business owners establish companies, they may plan your itinerary and show you what they prefer you to see. It is better that you visit places on your own, for only in this way can you truly ascertain the advantages and disadvantages a site may offer to your proposed business.

Investment Opportunities throughout the World

While most of the major population centers are dotted with hundreds of hundreds of companies whose chief business is travel and tourism, there are numerous opportunities in lands not generally recognized as being prime vacation destinations. Many of these places benefit from growing economies and are the tourist sites of tomorrow. Many are already enjoying increasing numbers of tourists, but there is plenty of potential for greater numbers of visitors. These are among the sites that entrepreneurs seeking to invest in travel and tourism should evaluate first.

Following is a list of twelve sites with some of the best potential:

The Azores – Centrally located between Europe and North America, the Azores, an island group that occupies a special place in the Portuguese Republic, offer numerous incentives for entrepreneurs interested in investing in the travel and tourism industry. The following incentives are available to eligible companies:

- A variety of programs of financial aid and subsidies are possible. These are based on the value of investment in fixed assets. Two particularly noteworthy programs are the European Regional Development Fund (ERDF) and the European Social Fund (ESF).

- The System of Incentives for Investment in Tourism (SIIT) is a program co-financed by the EFRD. The objective of SIIT is to develop the tourist sector. Incentives include direct financial grants for eligible enterprises.

Barbados – Already a well known tourist destination, Barbados is also an excellent site at which to establish a business because of the numerous incentives the government offers. Depending upon their specific operations, companies may be eligible for the following:

- Tax holidays for up to ten years.

- Low tax rates of 2.5% for businesses.

- Exemptions from local taxes on dividends, interest, fees, royalties, and management fees.

- Exemptions from import tariffs on production-related equipment such as computers.

- Cash grants for training.

- Subsidized space for facilities.

- The possibility of accelerated depreciation allowances.

The Republic of Ireland – In recent years, the Republic of Ireland, often referred to as simply Ireland, has developed into one of the finest spots for European investment. Along with an impressive financial sector, light manufacturing, and agriculture, tourism is a major component of Ireland's economy. To support economic expansion, the Irish government has enacted legislation providing for various incentives to entrepreneurs and investors. For those interested in travel and tourism, the Shannon Airport Customs Free Zone offers significant benefits. To qualify for a license to conduct business in the Free Zone, a company must show that its operations in some way contribute to the development or use of Shannon Airport. The most noteworthy incentive for qualified companies is reduced tax rates.

Madeira – Located in the eastern Atlantic, Madeira is developing into one of the European Union's most important international business centers. Madeira is actually a group of islands that enjoys a large measure of autonomy even though they are officially a part of the Portuguese district of Funchal. Madeira is fast becoming a site of finance, business, and travel. While incentives are available to a variety of different types of companies, entrepreneurs seeking to establish companies that can compete in the travel and tourist sector will likely find the greatest benefits in the Industrial Free Trade Zone near Canical. The following incentives are available to eligible companies operating within the zone:

- An exemption until 2011 from corporate taxes on income obtained from business conducted in the zone.

- An exemption from local taxes.

- An exemption from municipal property taxes on income derived from business conducted in the zone.

- An exemption from transfer, gift, and inheritance taxes in certain cases on the acquisition of real estate for purposes of setting up operations in the zone.

- An exemption from capital gains tax on the sale of fixed assets.

- An exemption from having to withhold taxes from the payment of royalties.

- An exemption from export quotas.

- An exemption from VAT and custom duties on imported goods and equipment, provided the goods are to be stored and/or transferred in the zone.

- An exemption from having to withhold tax from interest on loans from foreign banks and on bonds issued by companies. Borrowed funds, however, must be used for investment in the zone exclusively.

- Subsidies of up to 50% for the training costs of staff.

Malta – Positioned near the center of the Mediterranean between North Africa and Italy, the islands of Malta benefit from the major sea routes of the Mediterranean. The island nation also benefits from the government's commitment to supporting a growing economy through various incentives. The incentives are aimed at several sectors, including tourism – close to a million tourists visit the Maltese Islands every year – trade, manufacturing, international financial services, and ship maintenance services. The major incentives for eligible companies include:

- An exemption from local and municipal taxes.

- Special loans at low interest rates.

- Investment tax credits.

- Accelerated allowances for depreciation.

- Special allowances for costs related to export promotion.

- Training grants.

- Free repatriation in any currency to any country of profits, capital, dividends, etc.

Portugal – Since 1986 when Portugal entered the European Union, in the opinions of many international investors the nation has emerged as one of the continent's best places to invest. Noteworthy to entrepreneurs, tourism is one of the sectors in which foreign investment is especially encouraged. Incentives include:

- Under the Regional Incentive System, eligible companies investing in tourism, manufacturing, mining, and trade may qualify for cash grants and loans at reduced rates.

- Under SIFIT II, reduced-rate loans are available to promote projects in the tourist sector.

- Under SIFIT III, the benefits of SIFIT II are expanded, but most importantly, long-term repayable subsidies are provided to companies in the tourist sector. This program supports investment in facilities, including remodeling, re-conversions of hotels, restaurants, and various tourist attractions.

Puerto Rico – This island is a major tourist site, and although there are numerous companies devoted to the travel and tourism, new companies serving niche markets always have excellent potential. One of the most important benefits of establishing a company in Puerto Rico is the opportunity to conduct business as if the company was located within the United States, while at the same time enjoying the many incentives Puerto Rico offers. These incentives are potentially substantial, including:

- Corporations and individuals doing business in Puerto Rico are not subject to U.S. Internal Revenue Service laws. (See Section 9 of the Federal Relations Act.)

- Corporations enjoy federal tax credits on profits earned in Puerto Rico, after those profits are remitted to U.S. parent companies. (See Section 936 of the U.S. Internal Revenue Code.)

- Service industries and manufacturers are eligible for a 90% exemption from Puerto Rico taxes. Such exemptions may be in effect from ten to 25 years, depending upon the location of the company.

- Companies may be eligible to receive a 60% exemption from municipal fees, excise and various taxes for licenses throughout the time of the tax exemption.

- Companies may benefit from various worker training programs, which include wage subsidies of up to 50%.

- The Tourism Development Law, enacted in 1993 and designed to encourage investment of private tourism enterprises, provides for additional incentives:

- Enterprises can receive a ten-year exemption from various taxes on the island. Exemptions may be renewable for an additional ten-year period.

- Income and dividends from tourism enjoy a 90% exemption from taxes.

- A 50% tax credit for investments is possible for eligible projects.

- Loans can be guaranteed through the Tourism Development Fund.

• The Economic Development Administration (EDA) provides services for the promotion of business in Puerto Rico.

• The Caribbean Development Program provides various benefits to companies.

Seychelles – Located in the Indian Ocean, northeast of Madagascar, the 118 islands known as Seychelles are becoming an important stop for tourists from throughout the Eastern Hemisphere. Indeed, tourism is the mainstay of the nation's economy. To support tourism, as well as to promote other sectors of the economy, the government of Seychelles has enacted various incentives, including:

- No personal income tax.

- No withholding tax on dividends.

- 100% repatriation of capital and profits.

- Accelerated rates for depreciation.

- No wealth taxes.

- No gift taxes.

- No property taxes.

- No capital gains tax or death duties.

- No import duties on capital equipment.

- Low business tax rates of 15% with additional tax credits lowering effective rates to about 9%.

- For certain eligible companies, complete tax holidays.

Singapore – The Republic of Singapore is best known as a dynamic business center. In an effort to maintain the tiny nation's business energy, its leaders have enacted numerous incentives to attract investors and entrepreneurs. Because of Singapore's international trade – more than 5,000 international companies maintain offices in the nation – business travel is constant, and there is always a need for travel and travel-related services. Entrepreneurs can realize excellent benefits from the following incentives:

- An exemption of corporate tax for up to ten years on income that results from pioneer activity.

- A concessionary tax rate on income derived from qualifying activities.

- A tax rate of 10% on income arising from the provision of approved services in Singapore for a period of up to ten years. An extension of this initial period may be granted.

- A full or partial exemption of withholding tax on approved royalties.

- An exemption of taxable income, not to exceed 50%, of an amount equal to a specified percentage of new fixed capital expenditure.

- Special grants for worker training.

St. Kitts and Nevis – The two-island nation of St. Kitts and Nevis lies about a third of the way between Puerto Rico and Trinidad. Along with being the site of the only international financial center in the Caribbean, the island of Nevis offers offshore banking services and superb asset protection trusts. In addition of their interest to investors, the islands are becoming a tourist destination. Various incentives attract entrepreneurs, the most important being:

- No personal income tax.

- No gift taxes.

- No sales taxes.

- No estate taxes.

- Corporations may enjoy tax holidays from ten to 15 years, depending on the amount of value their operations provide to the islands.

- Eligible companies receive an exemption from import duties on parts, raw materials, and production materials.

- Hotel proprietors may benefit from the Hotel Aids Ordinance. This act provides that the gains or profits of a hotel of more than 30 bedrooms is exempt from income tax for a period of ten years. Hotels of less than 30 rooms may qualify for an exemption of five years.

- For companies registered with the Federation of St. Kitts and Nevis, full repatriation of all profits, dividends, and imported capital is guaranteed.

- Because St. Kitts and Nevis is a member of the Caribbean Common Market (CARICOM), companies enjoy duty-free access to other CARICOM countries.

- In accordance with the Lome Convention, St. Kitts and Nevis enjoys privileged access to the countries of the European Economic Union (EEC).

St. Lucia – Along with manufacturing and shipping, tourism is a growing sector of the island's economy. Significant legislation provides numerous incentives for businesses, including:

- Tax holidays for manufacturers for up to 15 years.

- Specific tax concessions for the hotel industry.

- No capital gains tax.

- No estate taxes.

- For eligible companies, concessions may be granted in regard to the depreciation of imports of machinery and equipment.

- St. Lucia has signed the Tax Information Exchange Agreement (TIEA) with the United States. This agreement permits investors to access "936" financing out of Puerto Rico for projects in St. Lucia.

- Subsidized rents for businesses at industrial parks operated by the National Development Corporation of St. Lucia.

- St. Lucia also benefits from several free-trade agreements, including The Caribbean Common Market (CARICOM), the Caribbean Basin Initiative (CBI), and CARIBCAN, a trade program of the Commonwealth Nations of the Caribbean.

Turkey – Turkey occupies a key position as a doorway to Eastern Europe and the states of the former Soviet Union, as well as Central Asia. As economic activity in the region expands, Turkey stands to benefit, serving as a waystation for businessmen and travelers. In the coming years, Turkey is likely to profit handsomely from the expanding economies of its neighbors. Anticipating these opportunities, the Turkish government has enacted an assortment of significant incentives for investors and entrepreneurs of eligible companies, including:

- An exemption from custom duties for imported machinery and equipment.

- Corporate tax exemptions, depending upon the type and location of the company.

- Exemptions from building, facilities, and construction taxes.

- Energy incentives for operations in Priority Development Regions.

- An exemption from VAT.

- Companies that operate in one of Turkey's five free zones enjoy a 100% exemption from all taxes.

The above countries comprise a small portion of those lands with business climates and laws favorable to entrepreneurs seeking to establish companies in the travel and tourism industry. While this list provides a starting point, meticulous research will uncover many other potential sites.

31

The world offers countless possibilities; it remains for the entrepreneur to identify the places and companies that offer the greatest potential returns on his investment.

While the world's economy will fluctuate in upcoming years, as it has throughout history, the trend toward the world growing smaller because of increasingly efficient methods of transportation is likely to continue. It is also likely that the travel and tourism industry will continue to expand, just as it has done for the past thirty years. The underlying reasons are simple, but significant: More people than ever desire to travel and they have the financial resources to do so. As travelers and destinations increase, so will the need for companies that offer travel and tourism services and products.

Why You Should Establish a Travel Agency

Entrepreneurs who are interested in the opportunities that may be found in the travel and tourism industry must be willing to visit potential investment sites. There is no other effective way to determine whether a site offers the elements and conditions that will ensure the profitability of the venture. Of course, this places the burden of travel costs squarely on the entrepreneur's shoulders. Imagine visiting several potential sites of investment on three or four different continents, and it quickly becomes clear just how costly traveling the world in pursuit of opportunity can become. Unless you have substantial resources, the search for potentially viable investment sites can rapidly devour the cash that will be needed for the investment. At the very least, extended travel will add significantly to your overall costs.

There is a better way: Establish a travel agency. Travel agencies can assume many forms. They can be set up as a sole proprietorship, a partnership, or a corporation. You can rent office space if you wish or you can work out of a spare room in your home. Agencies may book all kinds of travel, or they may specialize, arranging, for example, only cruises or vacation packages and tours.

No matter how big the agency is, or the type of travel services it markets, travel agents enjoy numerous benefits. While all of the benefits are noteworthy, the most important to the entrepreneur who seeks global investment opportunities is the reduced rates for travel.

Consider the following benefits you will receive as a travel agent:

- You will receive deep discounts on many of the trips you take, whether for business or pleasure.

- In most cases, whenever or wherever you travel, you will receive the lowest rates available.

- Because you are a travel agent, you will receive upgrades to better airline seats and hotel rooms.

- In many instances you will receive substantial discounts on hotels, restaurants, and tours. Depending upon occupancy rates and the time of year, some hotel discounts can run as high as 70%. In some restaurants you will be able to eat full-course meals for free.

34

- You will receive special low rates on rental cars.

- You will receive discounts for vacation packages at many resorts.

- You will receive discounts on tour packages.

- You will be able to take advantage of familiarization trips sponsored by resorts and cruise lines. In most cases the rates for these trips will be greatly reduced and in some cases the trips will be free. This is especially true if you supply the travel service provider with steady business.

- You will receive discounts for admission to resorts and theme parks.

- You may receive complimentary tickets to plays, stage productions, and special events.

The great value of travel discounts is that you are now able to visit various places around the world to determine their worth as potential sites for investment. Even if you are on a familiarization tour, which is designed to introduce you to the provider's services, there will always be an opportunity to spend some time away from the tour during which you can scout potential investments. You will truly be mixing business with pleasure.

In addition to the benefits above, travel agents enjoy numerous other benefits, including:

- As an entrepreneur, you will enjoy owning and operating a business.

- You will enjoy the tax benefits that come with business ownership.

- By establishing your own agency, you will be your own boss and not work for someone else.

- You will decide upon the location of your agency – whether you will rent office space or work out of your home. A home-based agency is probably best for most individuals who wish to use the agency as a means of travel in assessment of investment opportunities.

- As your own boss, you will set the hours you work. You will also be able to decide how much business you wish to do. Many home-based travel agents maintain their agency on a part-time basis.

- You will make decisions hiring staff.

- You will have the chance to control your own destiny.

Most people who are not involved in the travel and tourism industry have little understanding of the many benefits travel agents enjoy. For the entrepreneur who establishes an agency primarily to reduce his travel costs as he seeks investment options, the agency can be a superior tool toward the achievement of that objective.

Becoming a Travel Agent

In order to take advantage of the many benefits available to travel agents, you must establish a true agency. While you may set up a part-time agency that operates out of your home, if you wish to receive reduced rates and discounts for travel, you must book trips for clients. This is not as hard as it may first appear.

The typical entrepreneur already possesses many of the traits necessary to be a successful travel agent. Without question, you will need a variety of effective business skills. Sound business sense, a general knowledge of operating a company, and specific understanding of selling and arranging travel packages are essential. Many resources on how to start and operate a travel agency are available through Internet sources and bookstores. These references can help you get started, however, there are other ways to acquire the skills necessary to be successful in the industry.

Not too long ago, by far the best way to learn the necessary skills was to take an entry level position in an established agency, learn the "ropes," and gradually work your way up. The typical agent of those days learned from experience, often by assisting seasoned travel professionals.

While you can certainly enter the field that way even today, a more practical route through which you can acquire the necessary expertise is to take classes in travel and tourism management. Such classes are offered at many four- and two-year colleges, as well as many adult evening schools. To locate these classes, contact local colleges and evening schools or your local state board of education. There are likely to be many offerings not far from your home, especially if you live in or near a large town or a city.

Before signing up for any course, evaluate the program and instructor. Ideally, the program should be comprehensive and cover all aspects of the travel and tourism industry including:

- An overview of the industry that includes airlines, cruise lines, car rental firms, resorts, tours, accommodations at hotels, motels, inns, and bed and breakfasts, group travel, and business travel.

- Marketing plans through which to find clients.

- The strategies for selling travel services.

- The techniques for selling travel services.

- Information about ARC/IATAN status, and how you can obtain such status. (Only travel agents who enjoy ARC (Airlines Reporting Corporation) and IATAN (International Airline Travel Agency Network) status are able to book airline tickets. Agents who are not ARC/IATAN affiliated must work in conjuction with a host agency that is and which can book airline tickets. To obtain ARC/IATAN status you would need to formally apply to the organizations, and post a bond to ensure your reliability and safeguard the value of airline tickets.)

- The procedures for booking tickets, cruises, tours, etc.

- Information about the travel and tourism industry throughout the world.

- Information about the world's geography and prime travel sites.

- Information about political and social factors that might affect travelers in different parts of the world.

- The role of computers in the industry in general, and how they will be crucial to the effectiveness of your business.

The scope and focus of the program are certainly important, but no less important is the experience of the instructor. A class conducted by anyone other than a travel agent, or someone prominent in the travel and tourism industry, will not provide you with the first-hand experience that is crucial to your understanding of the industry.

An added consideration is the school's, or instructor's, connections with the travel and tourism industry. Schools or instructors who have close ties to travel agencies and providers can often be important resources, because of their ability to help you contact companies and individuals who can foster and promote your agency in the early-going.

40

Even though you may attend classes in travel and tourism management, most states in the U.S. – and also many other countries – do not require travel agents to earn special degrees. Only a few states in the U.S. require travel agents to register or obtain state certification. Some states and local governments, however, do have regulations that travel agents must follow and you should check with your attorney regarding any documents you may need to file. In most cases, such documents are little more than a formality.

Of the various types of travel agencies, the home-based agency is the most practical for the entrepreneur who wishes to use his agency primarily as a method through which to obtain reduced rates for personal travel. Because it operates from his home, the entrepreneur incurs low start-up costs and overhead, while still being able to realize the benefits of large agencies.

Remember, the purpose of your travel agency is to provide you with a means of receiving reduced rates for travel and accommodations. Once you establish the company, if you wish, you can hire individuals to handle the daily operations, which will free you to focus more on investment possibilities.

Character Traits Necessary for Successful Ventures

Successful entrepreneurs share many of the same traits. Consider how you measure up against the following entrepreneurial characteristics:

- Goal-oriented.

- Highly motivated.

- Determination.

- Resourceful.

- Creative.

- Ability to identify new ideas.

- Ability to find opportunities which others overlook.

- Perseverance.

- Ability to make decisions.

- Effective risk-taking.

- Effective skills in communication.

- Effective listening skills.

- Ability to evaluate circumstances and situations.

- Organization skills.

- Ability to adapt to changing conditions.

- A strong belief in themselves and their goals.

- Ability to motivate others.

- Ability to recognize and utilize the talents of others in the pursuit of goals.

Travel and tourism comprise one of the world's growth industries, offering entrepreneurs unique investment opportunities. Establishing a travel agency is one of the most effective methods of seeking, identifying, and taking advantage of these opportunities.

Types of Travel Agencies

While all travel agencies have much in common, they can be divided into several major types. In most cases, agencies are defined by the kinds of travel services they provide. The major types of agencies include:

- Full service agencies, which are capable of serving all of a client's travel needs. Full service agencies generally provide services to individuals, families, and businesses. Most offer vacation packages, tours, cruises, group travel, and business travel. The full service agency can provide airline tickets, car rentals, and accommodations.

- Commercial agencies serve the needs of companies and corporations, managing the travel needs of businesses. In some cases, they will book vacations and tours, but this is usually done only for the personnel of major companies and corporations.

- In-house agencies most often are branch offices of a travel agency, located within a corporate client's facilities. The in-house agency arranges travel for the client's personnel.

- Group agencies concentrate their operations on groups, frequently booking tours and cruises.

- Home-based travel agencies are usually small and owner operated. Most sell various travel services to individuals and families, and many are affiliated with large agencies which carry out bookings. Commissions from sales are split.

Operating a Home-based Travel Agency

Perhaps the most significant advantage of a home-based travel agency is that it permits the owner to set his own hours and work as much in the agency as he wishes. Because most home-based agencies are part-time enterprises, the owner is able to pursue other ventures. The income of the agency is determined by how much work the owner puts into it, however, he need not be a full-time operation to realize the various benefits travel agents enjoy.

Some home-based agencies are built into full-time businesses, and some eventually expand and move into office parks, but most do not. Many owners, however, prefer to keep their business small, yet they still receive reduced rates for travel and accommodations. Some of these owners establish and maintain their agencies primarily as a way to obtain travel benefits.

Home-based travel agents have various options of how to conduct business. Some build their companies into full-service agencies, which can manage all of their clients' travel needs from transportation to accommodations. Some concentrate their efforts on the public in general, while others sell services almost entirely to corporations and companies. Some nurture specialty markets, selling only cruises or tours, for example.

For those owners who wish to limit their operations, collaborating with a host agency is recommended. When working with a host agency, the home-based agent functions much like a representative of a big, full-service agency. Operating much like a partnership, this design permits the home-based agent to offer the services (in conjunction with the host agency) a large travel agency can provide yet he retains his independence. The home-based agent sells travel services, then contacts the host agency which makes the actual bookings for transportation, accommodations, tours, and car rentals. The host agency then shares the commissions it earns from bookings with the home-based agent. Thus, the home-based agent spends much of his time finding clients and selling travel services but does not arrange the actual bookings.

Many home-based agents work in collaboration with a single host agency; some work with a few. Because the home-based agent is an indepenent, he is free to work with whichever host agencies he finds most compatible with his needs and business goals.

There are several advantages the home-based gains when working with a host agency. Perhaps the most significant is that the home-based agent remains an independent contractor, who can choose which agencies with whom he wishes to work. This is an important factor because the relationship between home-based agent and host agency is often negotiable. The details of the actual working arrangement, for example, is left to the two parties. Some home-based agents act as little more than finders of clients, while others play a great role in marketing and selling services. The commission split is also negotiable, sometimes varying with the types of services sold.

No less important is the value of a host agency's ARC/IATAN status. ARC (Airlines Reporting Corporation) and IATAN (International Airlines Travel Agency Network affiliation are essential for travel agencies to book airline tickets. Only agencies that possess ARC/IATAN status can collect commissions paid on airline tickets. Although there are exceptions, most airlines are reluctant to work with home-based agencies, which they may believe are not secure or reliable enough to ensure the safety of their tickets. Consequently, most home-based agencies require the collaboration of a host agency to obtain tickets for them.

The relationship between home-based and host agency, therefore, is mutually beneficial. The home-based agent finds business for the host agency, and the host agency provides airline tickets and other services that the home-based agency may not be able to offer.

There are, of course, many services that home-based agents can offer to clients that do not require the involvement of a host agency. Many cruises and tours, for example, can be booked by home-based agents. If the home-based agent arranges for travel services independently, he receives the full commission. Moreover, many providers of cruises and tours are willing to work with home-based agents, provided the agent proves that he is reliable and can supply a steady stream of business.

While some home-based agents are content to work with a host agency, many others network with travel providers, including resorts, cruise lines, and hotels, which not only enables them to offer the packages of the providers to their clients, but also enables the agent to gain special incentives and benefits from the providers. When the travel agent regularly sends business to a particular resort, for instance, that resort may reward the agent with a discounted vacation package for himself and his family.

Most home-based travel agents build professional relationships with travel providers that are mutually beneficial. For most, such relationships are the most practical method of achieving success.

Finding Clients

Many home-based travel agents maintain part-time operations with some maintaining operations mostly as a means of enjoying the benefits bestowed by the industry. Entrepreneurs whose purpose in establishing a home-based travel agency is to obtain reduced rates for travel and discounts on accommodations are likely to limit the hours they spend selling travel services. For these individuals, their greatest source of clients will center around family, friends, neighbors, and colleagues. For many entrepreneurs, these sources alone can provide a substantial number of potential clients.

While the effective marketing of travel services is always essential, marketing becomes critical when attempting to sell services to a small group of potential clients. The key is to offer travel services that will appeal to the targeted clientele. If most of your family, friends, and colleagues are married and have children, offering family vacations and travel packages to resorts will likely be of interest to them. On the other hand, if you have many friends, business associates, and colleagues who are single, or are married but do not yet have children, offering weekend getaways to some of the islands of the Caribbean will result in more business than a package for a trip to Walt Disney World in Florida.

By far most of the people who establish travel agencies concentrate their efforts on selling travel services. Depending upon their skills and business acumen, some of these individuals go on to build thriving travel agencies. Some even expand and open branch offices.

While building a profitable travel agency is certainly noteworthy, particularly when one considers the numerous benefits the typical travel agent enjoys, one of the most important potential benefits often goes unnoticed. That benefit, of course, is using reduced rates for travel and accommodations as a method of visiting places throughout the world where investment in travel and tourism provides a unique opportunity.

Assessing the Right Investment Opportunities

Whenever one considers any investment, careful assessment and planning are vital. This statement assumes even greater importance when that investment is aimed at a foreign site where political and social systems, language, methods of conducting business, and tax laws vary. The need for meticulous evaluation becomes crucial.

The entrepreneur who seeks investments in the travel and tourism industry on the worldwide scale is invariably confronted by countless choices. This is due to the scope of the industry, as well as its rapid growth during the past 25 years.

In some places this growth has placed a strain on infrastructure and support industries. Some major city airports, for example, are already hard-pressed to manage the air traffic they now have efficiently, and the prospect for congestion is expected to worsen as more and more people fly for business and pleasure. This is despite the fact that many cities are expanding their airport facilities. Expansion simply can not maintain the pace with demand. For many cruises, reservations must be secured months in advance, and quality accommodations at top resorts are often booked a year or more ahead. The robust growth of the travel and tourism industry clearly offers innumerable opportunities to investors.

Because of such steady growth, however, obstacles abound. In some places, growth eventually slows because of inadequate infrastructure and facilities. Excessive congestion can quickly tarnish an otherwise desirable destination, leaving investors in the travel and tourism industry desperate for a positive return on their capital. Careful and attentive evaluation of any potential site is necessary to avoid the pitfalls and find the opportunities.

The industry is, indeed, broad and opportunity may be found just about anywhere travelers and tourists go. Entrepreneurs may choose from various ventures.

Depending upon the area, a variety of recreational activities may be offered, including boating, camping, mountain climbing, golf, hiking, swimming, fishing, and whitewater rafting. Note that these are just some activities and specific locales may support numerous others.

Sightseeing often comprises additional activities. A site may be an ideal spot for nature walks that highlight an area's lush forests and biodiversity, or its unique physical features, or perhaps its archeological treasures.

Shopping is a favorite of tourists, and entrepreneurs are always wise to explore the possibility of opening shops that either provide local handicrafts or necessities to travelers. Jurisdictions that maintain free zones where products can be manufactured under special incentives can offer exceptional opportunities for the entrepreneur who prefers production and then supplies local distributors.

There are also vast opportunities in the field of entertainment, including the production of musical events, celebrations, sporting events, festivals, and theater performances. Companies that offer complementary services to entertainment are also possible investment choices. Those companies that offer management services, ticketing, or security for major tourist events may work in the background but are often quite profitable.

Because travelers and vacationers always need places to stay, hotels, motels, and restaurants are major but potentially lucrative investments. Convention centers and resorts also fall in this category, as do second home developments.

Companies that provide the materials and supplies that hotels and restaurants require are still more potential investments.

Finally, the entrepreneur seeking investment in the travel and tourism industry should never underestimate the transportation sector. Once travelers arrive at a destination, they need to be able to move from place to place quickly, efficiently, and comfortably. From taxi services to shuttles to aircraft that can fly tourists to the various islands of an archipelago, transportation companies can realize relatively fast profitability.

While virtually all major destinations have companies offering numerous services for vacationers and business people, there are many niche markets that are waiting to be exploited. Moreover, there are many places throughout the world that are only now emerging as important destinations. It is at these places where the greatest opportunities may be found.

The task of the entrepreneur is to explore various sites and select those that are most likely to support investment. To find such sites and their opportunities, careful evaluation and planning are essential.

The Need to Look into the Future

The success of any company in the travel and tourism sector is ultimately dependent upon one crucial factor: the company provides a service (or services) to people who desire to travel to or visit a particular place. No matter how exotic or wondrous a place may be, unless people want to visit – for vacation, a getaway, sightseeing, etc. – or need to visit – business – a company will have trouble growing and the investment is likely to be a poor choice. The entrepreneur, therefore, who finds a site and decides to develop it assumes a huge task. It is much better to find a desirable place which already enjoys popularity and which is expected to grow in popularity in the future. Such a place will provide a solid foundation for potential growth.

While certainly desirable, growth can also have its drawbacks. A site must have the resources to sustain growth. Consider the spot which experiences rapid growth in tourism for a period of ten years but then begins to run out of available land and resources. Perhaps the water supply becomes strained. Or maybe streets, roads, and highways cannot handle the increasing congestion. Maybe the area's infrastructure becomes overwhelmed. The investor who just a few years earlier made a large capital commitment now finds himself in an area whose growth has stagnated and whose reputation as a prime destination has been sullied. At the least his investment is now tarnished and its growth uncertain. Careful analysis of the area before investment would have revealed the possible underlying pitfalls to growth. Perhaps this would result in the individual not making the original investment, or it might have led to an awareness of potential problems and plans to manage them.

Knowing the Community

Successful entrepreneurs leave little to chance when evaluating potential investments. They not only work hard to assess the actual investment, but they strive to understand the region and community as well.

Before committing to any investment, no matter how potentially profitable that investment might seem to be, they carefully consider the area. Will the community be supportive of the entrepreneur's idea? If the entrepreneur sees opportunity in the establishment of a specialty shop which can offer items to tourists, he must be certain that the community will accept his presence and the competition he will offer to local businesses. Even though the national government may encourage foreign investment through incentive plans, local leaders and community members may not be as welcoming. It is essential that the entrepreneur visit the proposed site, meet with local officials, and "get a feel" for the business environment. If he senses that his company will truly be welcomed, he should move ahead; if, however, he finds suspicion, distrust, or resentment, he might need to reconsider the true potential of this site.

Establishing a positive relationship with local officials is a vital step to the success of your investment. There will be many occasions where you will need to rely on individuals in the government to assist you in obtaining necessary documents, direct you to the proper authorities to answer your questions, or simply introduce you to fellow businessmen and suppliers.

The entrepreneur must also carefully assess the potential workforce of the area. Unless he intends to manage his investment himself, he will need to assemble a staff. Three questions are critical here:

- Does the local population include people who will be skilled enough to fill his staffing needs? If not, can the entrepreneur arrange for the necessary training in a cost-effective manner? In some places, as an incentive to attract foreign investment, the government provides subsidies for training.

• Does the local population speak English – or does the entrepreneur speak local dialects fluently? One should never underestimate the barriers to business different languages present.

• Will locals be willing to work for the wages the entrepreneur can pay? The reverse is also a necessary question. Will locals possess the education and work ethic necessary to earn their wages?

The answers to all of these and similar questions undeniably affect the overall profitability of a venture. When questions regarding the potential of a site arise, caution should be exercised.

Potential for Growth

After you have decided that an area may be a potentially successful site for investment in tourism and travel, you must determine if the market will grow sufficiently to support your investment. Market growth must be projected accurately.

ou must predict the rate of increase in tourism and how that increase will affect your venture. Little growth means that any growth of your business must come at the expense of your competition. Competing against established companies, however, is a difficult path to profitability. Of course, growing tourism helps to boost the success of those companies that meet the tourists' needs.

The area's support industries must also be assessed. Such industries include the number of hotels, motels, and restaurants, infrastructure such as airports, railroads, bus lines and roadways, and natural resources including lakes, beaches, mountains, and so on. Facilities including hospitals, security services, and governmental agencies whose objective is to foster travel and tourism are also essential. Together, these support industries and facilities will aid the growth of your investment.

You may find what at first blush is the ideal vacation spot, virtually unknown to the outside world. You can envision it as becoming a prime travel destination and, no doubt, in time it will. However, if the area is lacking in support industries, facilities, and services, it may take years for your initial investment to provide meaningful returns.

The Legal Environment

Any business operates within a legal framework. While entrepreneurs are likely to be familiar with the laws that govern the operations of business in their home country, they may not be familiar with the laws that apply to a different jurisdiction. Business laws vary, sometimes significantly from place to place, and you must be certain that you thoroughly review the laws that may affect your investment.

Before committing to any investment, you should consult an attorney who is familiar with the laws of the jurisdiction. In particular you must be fully knowledgeable of the basic business laws, incentives provided by government, possible grants, special laws that may apply to foreign investment, and laws that may affect the returns of your investment. You should also scrutinize exchange regulations.

Be cautious of making any commitments until you have carefully evaluated the legal framework that will govern your investment. All agreements should be in writing, and nothing of a legal nature should be left to interpretation or chance.

Your Role

A question with far-reaching implications is whether or not you will remain on site to manage your investment. Because there are so many investment opportunities in the travel and tourism industry around the world, this is not an easy question to answer.

You may simply buy securities through an offshore investment house, in which case the fund management will handle your assets, but if you invest in a business, your presence will, at least part of time, be required. If you are establishing a company, you may need to reside nearby. The amount of time you will need to be present will vary, based on the type of investment, whether you have partners, and the quality of the staff you can hire. Nonetheless it is likely that you will have to spend some time to ensure the proper start-up of your company.

Lifestyle, obviously, is a serious factor in your assessment. Establishing a company that provides wildlife tours of the local terrain may offer substantial potential, but it may also require that you directly manage the operation, at least in the early-going. However, if you find that the lifestyle you will have as a tour manager will not match the type to which you have grown accustomed and enjoy, the investment is probably not the right one for you. Being an absentee owner in a company at which your presence is demanded is a poor arrangement for success.

You must try to accurately project the amount of time you will need to spend with your investment. If the investment requires more time than you can provide, you will either need to hire more staff, which can be expensive and which will reduce your profits, or the success of your investment may falter. Many potential overseas investments fail because the investors failed to correctly consider the amount of time they would have to spend with their ventures.

Deciding on the Kind of Investment

The next step is to decide which type of company to establish or investment to make. While the travel and tourism industry can be dizzying in its complexity, niche markets are everywhere, limited only by the imaginations of entrepreneurs. Consider the following ideas:

- A shop selling island souvenirs to tourists.

- A shop selling pastries and regional delicacies to travelers.

- A manufacturing plant that takes advantage of free zone incentives and which produces specialty items aimed at resort vacationers.

- A restaurant adjacent to an airport.

- Shuttle service that can whisk tourists around island points of interest.

- A company that provides guide services to groups interested in visiting outland sites.

- A beauty shop that offers tourists all of the comforts of home in an island setting.

- A small motor boat rental company.

- A company that rents water sports equipment for scuba-diving, snorkeling, swimming, and fishing.

- A charter boat service for tourists who desire fishing for marlin, shark, and other gamefish.

- A company that offers financial management services for local firms.

- An insurance company that specializes in offering policies to companies that provide tourist and travel services.

- A bed and breakfast inn overlooking the mountains and from which hiking and bicycling tours can be organized.

- A hotel or motel at a prime site. Note that these facilities need not be big to be profitable, particularly if they enjoy a prime location. A small beach that has been overlooked for years, for example, on the outskirts of a resort city can be the site of future development. Those who establish a presence there first are likely to profit handsomely.

- A night club offering island music, food, and entertainment.

- A consulting service that offers advice to fledgling local businesses.

- Investment via partnership into an already established company, the goal being to expand the company's products and services.

- A local travel agency, a branch of your home office.

Two factors that play a large part in the success of any venture are location and timing. A prime location and investing at a time travel and tourism in an area is growing are basic to eventual profitability.

Inexperienced entrepreneurs often look for high-profile investments. While these are easiest to find, they are also the ones that face the strongest competition. Finding a niche market requires meticulous research but often presents a greater profit potential, both for the short- and long-term.

The Need for Flexibility

The search for the right investment in the right jurisdiction can be an arduous task. It is easy to become

65

impatient and select a site and investment that may, on the surface, appear to be a wise choice, but under meticulous evaluation proves to be mediocre at best.

To reduce the possibility of making a decision on incomplete information, you should not place yourself under a time limit. Rather than beginning your search with a firm target date – for example, you set aside a period of six months in which to find an investment site – conduct your search within the framework of seeking the *best* investment. This will encourage you to compare various investments.

When comparing investments, be sure to use the same criteria. Varying criteria will undermine your process of evaluation. At the least, you should evaluate any potential investment site according to the following:

- Location.

- Legal environment.

- Business environment.

- Social environment.

- Workforce.

- Infrastructure.

- Travel and tourism companies already established.

- Potential competing firms.

- Prospects for future growth of the general economy in the region.

- Prospects for future growth of the travel and tourism industry in the area.

- Prospects for the growth of your investment.

- Amount and quality of support industries.

- Amount and quality of support governmental and quasi-governmental agencies.

- Other factors that might be unique to the region.

Collecting Information

Gathering accurate data is a critical component of the process of identifying potentially successful investments in the travel and tourism industry. By far the best method is to visit the site and speak with government officials, local leaders, bankers, business owners, and residents.

Prior to meeting with officials, create a list of questions that will help you to ascertain the business, legal, and social climates that will inevitably affect your investment. These questions, while tactful, should be specific and help you to uncover the reality of the site and not just "appearances." Avoid questions that can be answered with a simple yes or no and instead ask questions that require explanations. Following are some sample questions:

For the government official:

- How does the government view foreign investment? (An appropriate response would be to encourage it.)

- In what ways does government treat foreign business owners differently than businesses owned by nationals? (Ideally, there should be no difference.)

- How do tax laws treat foreign investment. (Concessions are a plus, and there should be no penalties.)

- What tax incentives are available to investors? (Many sites offer numerous incentives from tax holidays to reduce rates.)

- What other special incentives are available? (Perhaps subsidies for training staff, or reduced costs for facilities can be negotiated.)

- How does the government promote or foster travel and tourism? (There should be some sort of nationally-sponsored advertising campaign.)

- What is government doing to make sure that infrastructure keeps pace with the growing numbers of visitors? (Plans should be in place that help to continually modernize airports, roads, bridges, rails, and telecommunications.)

- What programs are in place to assist new businesses in their establishment and operations? (At the least there should be an agency that will reduce the amount of bureaucracy that would otherwise mire a company in red tape.)

For local leaders:

- What is the attitude of local businesses and residents toward foreign investment? (It should be positive and supportive.)

- How do local leaders feel about foreign investment? (They should encourage it.)

- How might the local government support the formation of your business? (It should be willing to do all it can to assist you, for example, providing contacts with suppliers, builders, etc. It should also help to streamline applications and the obtaining of any necessary permits, certificates, and licenses.)

For bankers:

- How willing is the bank to loan money to foreign investors? (They should be willing, provided the venture has a reasonable chance for success.)

- How willing is the bank to loan money to start-ups? (They should be willing to loan money to investors seeking to establish a business.)

- What special loan rates, if any, does the bank offer new businesses? (Even if they do not offer special programs, they might be willing to negotiate special rates with you.)

- What is the general fiscal attitude of the bank's management? (A moderately conservative, pro-growth management can be good for business. Such management will be supportive of the business community but will be cautious of over-extending the bank's financial reach.)

- How strong is the bank? How much reserves does it maintain? (The bank should maintain an adequate level of reserves in balance of its outstanding loans.)

- What are the prevailing interest rates? (They should be acceptable.)

- What are the procedures for securing credit? (They should be relatively straight-forward without special contingencies or requirements.)

For the business owners:

- What is their impression of the government's attitude toward business? (They should report that the government supports business.)

- How does government assist business? (Government should provide a framework in which business can operate in as free a climate as possible.)

- What is their opinion of foreign investment? (They should welcome it.)

- How do they perceive the area's infrastructure? Is it modern and of high quality? Does it support the needs of business? How might it be improved to support business even better? (The infrastructure should, at the minimum, provide for the needs of business in the areas of telecommunications and transportation.)

- How would they rate the area's support services – police and security, health care, related businesses and suppliers – excellent, adequate, or inadequate, and why? (Support services should be adequate.)

- Do they feel that the area's travel and tourism sector is capable of growth and why? (They should feel that there is room for expansion.)

For residents:

- What is their opinion and feeling regarding foreign investment? (They should welcome it.)

- What do they consider the general economic conditions of their area to be? (They should feel relatively upbeat about them.)

- What factors are the most important factors that affect the local and regional economies? (The more positive factors the list the better.)

- What role do they feel government plays in the economy, most especially in the support of business? (Their remarks here should support what government officials tell you.)

- If they could project what the economy will be like in a year, three years, and five years, what do they feel will transpire? (The opinions of ordinary people can often shed much light on a topic.)

These types of questions can reveal much about the place in which you are considering investing. Whenever asking questions, always ask politely. Avoid any semblance of confrontation or interrogation. Listen attentively and take notes. If you are unclear about an answer, or if the answer begets another question, pursue the topic.

Try to learn as much as you can. Only in this way will you be able to gather enough information to make a truly informed decision. You should travel not as a tourist but as an observer.

Some individuals find that creating a questionnaire is helpful. The questionnaire, which should cover the material in the previous questions, can be distributed to several people and the results easily tabulated and compared.

Questionnaires do have drawbacks, however. While a questionnaire can generate a substantial amount of data, it cannot provide the insight that a personal interview can. When you speak with people directly, body language can become as informative as words. A person can tell you one thing, but his body may be telling you another. This can be especially important when dealing with government administrators who might be under pressure to encourage investment, even though the promises they make have little official support behind them.

Because choosing an investment that has strong potential for success can be such a demanding objective, the investor is well advised to gather as much information from as many sources as he can, compare and evaluate all the data thoroughly, and only then decide whether or not the proposed investment is the right one.

Financial Resources and Raising Capital

Like any business, establishing a company in the travel and tourism industry requires capital. Unless you intend to fund your investment alone, you will need to secure financial backing.

Before you approach institutions and individuals about investing in your enterprise, you must have a good idea of how much money you will need. You must anticipate the overall costs the operation of your business will incur as well as your likely income. While it is difficult to be precise with these numbers, you must try to project as accurately as possible what your expenses and revenues will be, because this will help you to determine how much funding you will require. This will also indicate to potential lenders and investors that you have carefully considered the financial needs of your business, which in turn will help them to form a positive impression of you.

Try to be as thorough as possible with your financial projections. Include all potential expenses and add an additional 20%. When you project your expected income, avoid too much optimism and temper your numbers with a healthy dose of realism. Remember, of even the best plans, the unexpected happens and things go wrong.

There are many sources of funding and you should consider all of them. The following are among the most common and practical:

- Personal assets.

- Banks and other financial institutions.

- Funds from friends, relatives, and associates. (Perhaps the company you establish will be a partnership.)

- Government loans.

- Regional and local development funds.

While in most cases you will need to invest some of your own money, the amount will vary, depending upon the type of investment and the site of the investment. Some jurisdictions require a rather large initial monetary commitment by the investor, particularly if he or she is a non-resident, yet others place few restrictions on the nature or composition of the investment.

Personal Assets

Few business ventures are begun without some of their founder's assets. Although you will probably need to commit some of your own money to the establishment of a business in the travel and tourism industry, you should look for ways to limit the commitment of your personal funds. Limiting the actual dollar among of your investment by securing loans from banks, cash from partners, or subsidies and grants from the government will reduce the risk to your personal assets. Still, you will have to use some of your money, for potential backers will be reluctant to spend their money on your venture if you appear unwilling to risk some of your own funds.

Whenever you are investing money in any enterprise, never commit more than you can afford to lose. Even ventures that might seem to have an exceptional chance for success and profitability should be viewed conservatively when it comes to the amount of your own money you invest. Keep in mind that unforeseen events can occur that can rapidly change the prospects of any venture from success to failure. Sometimes, unfortunately, the best laid business plans go awry, not because of the poor planning or negligence on the part of the owner but because of situations that are truly out of his control. You must, therefore, always be prepared to lose your investment.

Given such possibilities, it makes sense to commit the smallest amount of your own assets as you can. If a local bank requires that you supply 20% of the start-up costs necessary to the establishment of a new business, you should commit that 20% but no more, unless there is a powerful reason for doing so. Perhaps you can enjoy a substantially greater tax benefit by using more of your own funds, but such situations must always be balanced against each other and you should choose the alternative that best leads to the achievement of your objectives.

Most entrepreneurs have various options for using their assets for investment. Perhaps you can use savings. If this is the case, be sure not to use more than you can afford to lose. Tapping funds set aside for retirement is generally an unwise strategy, as is taking cash that has been set aside for a child's education, a downpayment for a new home, or other worthy purpose.

Borrowing money to make the initial investment is also generally unwise. Assuming a second mortgage on your home to raise cash for investment is a dubious strategy. Other examples of ways not to raise cash include taking personal loans and credit card advances. Not only will the interest payments erode your income and any early profits, but lending institutions may look unfavorably on loaning you money because of your debt. If they are willing to loan you money, it is likely to be at a higher rate of interest, which will offset their losses should you eventually be unable to pay them back.

A possibility for raising the cash necessary for investment is to sell stocks or bonds. Whenever you consider securities to raise money for investment, however, you must be aware of the possible capital gains consequences and the overall effect the sale will have on your tax obligations. If selling stocks or bonds results in a significant increase in your tax obligations, the strategy is probably the wrong one.

While you should be ready to rely on some of your own assets in your investment, you should also seek ways to limit the exposure of your assets to unexpected, negative occurrences. In short, use your money to get started and then try to secure the financial backing of others to expand.

Banks

Banks are an essential component of the business community, and most entrepreneurs seek to obtain financing from banks first. Most businesses grow through the use of loans, which provide the money for expansion. Regions in which banks and other financial institutions are uncooperative when it comes to making business loans generally have weaker economies than those in which banks actively support companies and the business community.

The following are attributes of banks that can be expected to support your venture:

- The bank, through its policies and actions, promotes the growth of private enterprise within the local region.

- The bank has a positive vision for the future economic growth of the area.

- The bank openly encourages the travel and tourism industry.

- The bank is a ready source of financing for businesses in general and for companies in the travel and tourism industry specifically.

- The bank provides services aimed at travelers and tourists.

- The bank is interested in the expansion of the travel and tourism industry and exhibits this interest through special loan concessions and services.

- The bank's officers and staff understand the travel and tourism industry and its impact on the community.

- The bank's officers and staff give a high priority for working with companies in the travel and tourism industry.

If the site in which you are considering investing is not yet a prime tourist attraction, and you find that the local bankers are not fully aware of the economic potential and benefits of a growing travel and tourist sector, you may take it upon yourself to help them understand the positive impact. Frank discussions can help bankers to understand how encouragement of travel and tourism firms can not only add to the local economy but also to their bottom line, making them more willing to consider providing your venture with special loan rates.

Funds from Friends, Relatives, and Associates

An important source of funds for many investors includes their friends, relatives, and associates. In some cases these individuals will assume the role of a partner –the percentage of the venture owned by the partners is determined by the amount of their financial commitment – but in many cases individuals providing money for the enterprise will remain in the background, assuming the role of "silent" partners. These people are not interested in the day-to-day running of the venture but rather are seeking a sound investment with steady, long-term returns.

The terms of any financial arrangement with others should be clearly detailed in documents composed by attorneys with business expertise. Moreover, your attorney should be familiar with the laws of the jurisdiction in which you are establishing your business. Agreements should be explained fully so that all parties understand the terms and conditions. Amounts, terms, rates, returns, and payoffs should be clearly detailed. Implications and contingencies should be anticipated and addressed, and nothing should be left to individual interpretation. All contracts, agreements, and documents should be filed with the appropriate authorities.

Friends, relatives, and associates can be an excellent source of financing for your venture. However, as with any type of financing, you must recognize that the money comes with expectations and obligations.

Government Loans

In an effort to encourage foreign investment, some countries have legislation that provides government loans to fledgling companies. The loans may take many forms, including:

- Loans aimed at start-ups.

- Loans designed for companies in the travel and tourism sector.

- Loans designed for specific enterprises – for example the building or renovating of hotels or motels.

- Loans for specially designated companies at reduced rates.

- Loans for companies that are located in specially designated areas of the country.

- Loans for companies that operate in free zones.

- Loans for companies that promise to hire members of the local population.

- Loans for specific activities – for example the training of a local workforce.

- Loans for the purchase of equipment.

- Loans for the building of facilities.

- Loans for the expansion of an existing company in the travel and tourism sector.

You should always investigate the possibility of securing special government loans. You can learn about these from the local business association, area officials, and government investment liaisons.

As with the securing of any loan from any source, you must be certain that you fully understand the assumptions and conditions of the loan. This can sometimes be tricky when negotiating with representatives of foreign governments whose ways of doing business are unfamiliar. The help of an attorney experienced with the business procedures of the host land is critical.

Regional and Local Development Funds

Similar to government loans are regional and local development funds designed to foster the growth of both new and established companies. Such funds may take the form of loans, subsidies, or grants. (Grants can be especially useful because they do not have to be paid back.) Funds from these sources may be aimed at specific operations of a business – for example, a loan for the purpose of purchasing computers and other technology, or a grant to help pay for the upgrading of a company's telecommunication system – or they may be general in scope – a subsidy for facilities.

Venture Capital Firms

Venture capital firms are one of the first sources many new entrepreneurs consider for obtaining financing for their companies. These entrepreneurs do not realize that most venture capital firms are quite specialized in the types of companies they choose to finance. Most seek companies that have high growth potential, typically with the capability to generate a 35% to 50% annual return on investment. These are numbers that few start-ups can attain, particularly in the travel and tourism sector. Because of the desire for high rates of return, many venture capital firms seek companies that are in the technology sector or are developing innovative new products with significant appeal.

While entrepreneurs can certainly contact venture capital firms in their attempt to raise funds, most will have a better chance of obtaining support by approaching the smaller companies, which can be more interested in backing a start-up in the travel and tourism industry. Even then you should not be disappointed if you are turned down, because most venture capital firms tend to look for emerging companies in fields that can generate a fast and high return. Despite the fact that companies in the travel and tourism industry may not fit the criteria of venture capital firms, they nonetheless can provide steady growth and solid returns.

The Need for Accurate Record-keeping

Whenever you raise capital or secure financial backing for your enterprise, you must keep accurate records. This is essential for the proper payment of taxes, including both short- and long-term capital gains.

Your accountant should be familiar with the tax laws of the jurisdiction in which you are investing, which are likely to be different than the ones you are familiar with at home. Poor record-keeping can result in mistakes that can lead to heavy tax penalties. In cases of severe faulty record-keeping, a company's operations can be so hampered that its success will be jeopardized.

Your Business Plan

Before anyone – a banker, business associate, friend, or relative – will invest money in your venture, he or she will want to know precisely what you intend to do with it and what kind of return can be expected. Unless you can show that your enterprise has a reasonable chance of succeeding, it is unlikely that you will be able to convince people to investing it. This is where a sound business plan becomes essential.

Virtually all successful companies have a business plan. Even the simplest plan addresses such topics as a company's ownership, management, objectives, general operations, products and services, estimated costs, revenues, and financial resources. Lacking a realistic and detailed business plan will severely undermine your chances of securing funding from banks and other financial institutions.

An effective business plan is written in clear, simple language and includes facts and concise information. Following is a typical structure for a business plan:

- Objectives: This section of your plan explains what you expect your company to achieve.

- Ownership: This part of your plan explains who owns your company.

- General Operations: This describes how your company will operate.

- Products/Services: This explains what your company will sell.

- Potential Market: This section of your plan describes to whom you hope to sell your products and/or services, and why the individuals in this market will buy what your company is offering.

- The Competition: This part of your plan details competing companies and how you expect to prosper.

- Management: This section describes who will run your company.

- Finances: This part of your business plan projects at least three years of your anticipated income and expenses.

- Financial Resources: This part includes all of your potential sources of income. (The people you approach for financing are always impressed when they see that they will not be the only ones investing in your company.)

- Special Relationships: This includes any contacts or agreements with other companies, suppliers, or government agencies that might be helpful in the establishment of your company.

One caution in writing your business plan: Stick to the facts. Avoid overstatement, overly optimistic scenarios, and specious projections. Experienced lenders and investors can quickly see through exaggeration and will think less of you and your company.

A business plan does not need to be excessive in length or detail, however, it should highlight and explain all pertinent aspects of your business. In short, a good business plan provides the reader with an informative summary of your vision for your company and how you hope to make that vision a reality.

A thoughtful, well-written business plan can secure the financing you need to establish your company and ensure its growth. Because few companies can succeed without solid financial backing, you must place financing high on your list of start-up priorities.

Building Your Investment through Marketing

Investing in a company that provides travel services is an exciting and challenging venture. If your investment takes the form of establishing a new business, you will need to plan carefully and consider the various obstacles that can stand in the way of your company becoming a success. It makes little difference where your company is located; the steps to eventual profitability for any company are much the same.

Most new companies fail within the first three years. Reasons abound for the high failure rate, ranging from poor location and insufficient resources to inexperienced management and ineffective marketing. There are, indeed, many more reasons for a business to fail than for it to succeed. Assuming that the business has been established in a prime location and that financial resources are adequate, the most prominent reason for failure becomes poor management. Fortunately, there is much you, as the owner, can do to ensure that your business is managed effectively.

While you may manage the business yourself, most entrepreneurs who invest in companies in other countries are not able to manage the company on site. They may be committed to other enterprises most, or at least part, of the time. They may have other foreign as well as domestic investments. They may need to devote much of their time to their travel agency, and/or the overseeing of still more investments or companies. For such men and women, time is a valued commodity, and the establishment of a company or investment site takes precedence over managing it. After establishing a company, such individuals typically enlist the help of local staff to manage it. Depending upon the caliber and experience of that management, the enterprise can go on to become quite successful even when the owner exercises control from another location.

There are obvious advantages to hiring managers from the local population, including:

- One, they speak the language of the area, most importantly dialects and special phrases that you, as an outsider, might not fully understand.

- Two, they are likely to understand the business practices of the area, including the customary methods of bargaining.

- Three, they are more likely to be trusted by the people who comprise your potential market.

- Four, they are more likely to be skilled in dealing with local bureaucrats, politicians, and other businessmen.

These are major advantages. Of course, these benefits evaporate if the individuals you choose to manage your company lack business experience, are not trustworthy, or are unreliable. To ensure that their management team is capable of operating their company effectively, many international entrepreneurs either remain on site or visit often, particularly during the start-up phase of the company. Their presence can be a stabilizing force and their expertise can help to establish routines and methods that will lead to a successful venture. Even if the management team you assemble is of the highest quality, you should visit your company regularly and remain in close contact via phone, fax, and computer.

Your presence during your new company's early stages can also be beneficial to the establishment of good relationships with local authorities, suppliers, and other business owners. Building good relations and mutual respect can help secure a position of top ranking for your company among the area's businesses.

Attending to Details

Whether you take an active part in the start-up of your company, or you delegate the responsibility to others, a variety of details must be attended to. Overlooking even minor details can lead to problems later.

In establishing your company, you must address the following:

- Secure the proper facility in a prime location.

- Obtain the necessary, up-date-equipment.

- Invest in technology that can give your company a competitive edge.

- Designate resources to pay for any renovations or remodeling that might be necessary.

- Obtain furniture, decorations, etc.

- Appropriate resources to pay for the costs for operations, including: mortgage/rent, utilities, insurance, communications, postage, publications, licenses, and miscellaneous fees.

- Allot resources to pay for employees.

- Allocate resources to pay for office supplies, materials, office upkeep such as janitorial services, etc.

- Plan for attorney, accounting, and other professional services.

- Arrange for advertising and promotion.

Attention to the details promotes a company's operations and helps to lead to profitability. The entrepreneur/owner can foster the development of his business by setting a tone that encourages productive and efficient work from his staff.

Developing a Marketing Plan

Without an effective plan for marketing its products and services, the best run company will have trouble achieving success. Earnings will be flat and growth will be slow or nonexistent. A sound marketing plan is crucial for the success of any business.

In its simplest definition, the purpose of a marketing plan is to make potential customers aware of your company's offerings. Marketing, however, includes several vital components:

- Planning

- Researching

- Packaging

- Promoting

- Advertising

The components of marketing all help to build an image of your company and the products and services it offers. An effective marketing plan is thorough and goal-oriented. Indeed, any initiative, idea, or project that can help to sell the services or products of a company should be addressed in its marketing plan. To develop a comprehensive marketing plan you should consider the following:

- Identify the potential customers of your company's products or services. Through careful research, you must determine who they are, where they live, what their general income is, and what their needs are. Especially consider why they would potentially buy your products or services.

- Determine who your competition will be and identify their strengths and weaknesses. Perhaps some of your competitors have been long established in the area and enjoy a large amount of customer loyalty. Also try to find the weaknesses of your competitors. Maybe your competitors have, over time, lost sight of the importance of focusing on their customers' needs, or no longer offer quality merchandise or professional, considerate service. Such points can provide an opening for your company to establish itself.

- Develop a promotional plan that makes your products and services prominent in the minds of potential customers.

- Create an advertising program that taps all of the major media outlets that are likely to reach your potential customers – newspapers, magazines, telephone, direct mail, billboards, TV, radio, and the Internet.

- Implement company policies and procedures that treat customers professionally and with consideration. Create a climate in which customers feel that you genuinely appreciate their business. Such an atmosphere encourages them to return and builds customer loyalty.

• Foster positive relations with area business leaders, public servants, and politicians. Such contacts can lead to free publicity and support in important places.

• Join or make contributions to local community service and charitable groups. This will not only introduce your company to people but also foster good will.

• Strive to build strong relations with customers and suppliers. This is essential for major accounts. Along with providing quality services and products, sending thank-you notes, and cards for birthdays, anniversaries, etc. can impress people with your consideration and remind them of your business.

Assessing Your Target Market's Potential

In the broadest sense, a market may be defined as all of the potential buyers of a product or service. Depending upon what is for sale, markets can be large and include various types of buyers, or they can be quite specific, focusing on only certain groups or limited segments of the population. Markets are comprised of individuals who possess the desire or need to buy a product or service and also the ability and willingness to purchase. Although the market for a venture in the travel and tourism industry is limited to travelers and vacationers, this can be a very large pool of potential customers.

Because the scope of this market is so vast, and the individuals that comprise it have varying needs, goals, and desires, you cannot expect all members of the group to be interested in your products or services. You must identify those that will be interested and target them with your marketing plan.

There are three important steps to target marketing:

- You must differentiate between the various subgroups of tourists and travelers. These subgroups, or segments, have diverse attitudes, outlooks, and desires. Understanding what the various segments desire can help you to formulate a successful marketing plan.

- You must identify the segment, or segments, that will most likely be interested in your products or services and target them directly by tailoring the market plan to appeal to their interests.

- You must develop and refine your products and services so that they satisfy the needs of the targeted segments.

Understanding market segmentation is essential to developing an effective marketing plan. Since the needs and desires of all members of the travel and tourism market are too diverse to desire any one product or service, identifying those individuals who are likely to be interested allows a company to focus the advertising and promotion of its products and services to specific people. The potential for selling is thus increased.

The objective of segmenting the market into clearly identifiable groups whose members have shared needs is to delineate those characteristics that will help you to design a marketing plan that will most effectively meet the needs of the group's members. Efficient market segmentation can help you to realize various benefits, including:

- Focusing effort and money on specific markets that offer the greatest potential for buying your products and services.

- Creating products and services that satisfy demand.

- Deciding upon the proper advertising media, which will help you to most effectively reach your market.

- Determining promotions that have the greatest chances to be successful.

Once you have segmented the overall travel and tourism market in your area, you are ready to design a comprehensive marketing strategy. The development of a sound marketing strategy is based upon several factors, including:

- Individual – age, occupation, education, income.

- Family characteristics – marital status, size of family, age of children.

- Geographic considerations – home, place of origin, destination.

- Reasons for travel – vacation, business, pleasure.

- Types of establishments visited – hotels, motels, restaurants, nightclubs, amusements, entertainment, shops, tours, sightseeing.

- Transportation variables – type of transportation, length of trip, season in which the trip is taken, travel party (individual or with group).

Careful consideration of the above factors will make it clear that many of the factors overlap. It thus becomes essential that the market is divided into segments as accurately as possible. Inaccurate segmentation will undermine your efforts at designing an effective marketing plan because the initial assumptions will be invalid.

Assessing individuals according to the factors will also help you to accurately note trends, general desires, and needs. This will aid you in categorizing travelers and identifying various groups.

Accurate segmentation is critical to your marketing efforts, because it can help you to concentrate on the groups that will be most likely interested in your products and services. This will enable you to draw detailed profiles of these individuals, helping you to focus your marketing efforts.

Without question, understanding why the individuals in your target groups travel can be some of the most useful information. People travel for a variety of reasons. While business, vacation, visiting friends, sightseeing, recreation, and entertainment are among the most common, there are other reasons as well, including traveling for medical purposes, personal fulfillment, seeking property to relocate, or education. Many people travel for more than one reason and purpose, and many people, while realizing some reasons they travel, may not be aware of others. A good example here is the couple that enjoys visiting tourist sites around the world for sightseeing, but in fact gains deep personal satisfaction in learning about other people and cultures and enjoys sampling foods in local restaurants.

Needs can be difficult to identify and only careful study and evaluation will result in your results being relatively accurate. Still, because most people have more than one reason for traveling, meticulous assessment is likely to lead you to the reasons most of the people of a particular segment travel. Such understanding can help you to further focus your marketing plan.

After segmenting the travel market in your area, and after careful evaluation of the needs of the individuals in various segments, still other factors must be weighed before you commit substantial resources to a marketing plan aimed at a particular group. These include:

- The size of the group. Is it large enough to warrant an investment of marketing resources?

- The factors that will determine whether or not you can reach the group via advertising and promotion? For example, if the group is too difficult to reach with your message, your resources might be better spent elsewhere.

- The spending capacity of the segment. Will the individuals in the group have the necessary funds and be willing to spend money on your products or services?

- Your ability to satisfy the desires and needs of the group through your products and services. You may be able to reach the group, they may have cash to spend, but your products or services may not satisfy their needs. In this case, your marketing plan will be one of unrealized potential.

Gathering Information for Marketing

The effectiveness of any marketing plan is based upon information. Accurate data provides the foundation on which sound marketing decisions can be made. There are numerous methods for collecting information about potential customers, however, before accepting any information you must consider several questions, including:

- Who gathered the information? Are they reliable, unbiased, and reputable? A group of scientists commissioned by a major tobacco company, for example, would not be a reliable source for facts about the deleterious effects of smoking. Similarly, a commission assembled by a government agency whose purpose is to attract foreign investment might not be reliable in predicting a region's future economic growth.

- Why was the information gathered? What purpose did the collectors of the data have? Were they simply collecting information for businessmen to use, or were they pursuing an agenda that might cause some facts to be viewed with skepticism?

- When was the information gathered? Recent information is always better than old information.

- What methods were used to collect the information? Were the methods and procedures of collection adequate and thorough? How was information collected? Telephone samplings? Questionnaires? Random interviews in public places? Were samples truly random, or were they conducted during a particular time of the day with a certain part of the population? Randomly calling people during the workday at home is likely to reach people who do not work. This would eliminate a rather large number of people whose attitudes regarding a variety of subjects might be quite different than those interviewed.

- Is the information clear and to the point? Are there variances in definitions? A tour, for example, must mean the same to you as it does to the information gatherers.

- Are there any inconsistencies, errors, or omissions that might indicate the data collection was incomplete, sloppy, or mistake-prone? Such findings could imply that the information, on the whole, is inaccurate and therefore of little use. At the least, it would suggest caution in using the data.

These and similar questions must be raised before you accept information from which you launch a marketing plan aimed at a specific segment of potential customers. In seeking information, you should consider various sources.

Government publications should be your starting point. If there is a government agency which has provided services that have helped you with your investment, it is likely that its staff can supply you with publications containing pertinent information you can use in marketing. These publications might be produced by a national, a state (or provincial), or a local governmental unit. Moreover, many of them will contain sources that you can contact for additional information. You can also contact governmental agencies whose departments foster foreign investment. Such groups can undoubtedly provide substantial information.

Universities and colleges are usually sources of a great many studies and publications, many of which can shed light on society in general as well as on specific groups. Such works can be sources of prime information.

In many locales, private organizations produce numerous publications containing an assortment of information. Chambers of Commerce and business associations are frequently providers of helpful data, as are consumer groups.

Of course, you can always collect information yourself. You may speak with local business owners, politicians, and individuals about the buying habits of people in certain groups, however, you must be careful that your questions are focused and that the data you obtain is reliable.

After you have collected data from several sources, you must analyze the information. Always compare information from various sources to make sure that the facts you have obtained are in agreement. If you find discrepancies in two sources, compare them against a third and a fourth. As trends and major points emerge from the data, try to support them with facts from several sources. Only when facts are confirmed can you be relatively certain that they are valid. At this point they may serve as parts of the foundation on which you will build your marketing plan.

Essentials of a Marketing Strategy

There are four essentials of any marketing strategy:

- Products/services

- Promotion

- Price

- Distribution.

While each variable is a distinct factor in a marketing plan, they are interrelated. Moreover, because your company can control these variables, you have great flexibility in designing an effective marketing plan.

Products and services, of course, are at the heart of any company's operations. Without desirable products or services, promotion, price, and distribution become meaningless because customers are not interested in what you have to offer.

Assuming a company has desirable products and services, promotion then becomes a crucial factor. Promotion, which includes advertising, is the means through which a company can bring its products and services into the awareness of potential customers. Your company may offer a truly unique and exciting European tour, but if no one knows about it, you will have few customers.

Desirable products and services that are effectively promoted can still garner poor sales if their price is too high, however. Unless you can offer fair value to travelers and tourists, it is unlikely your company will reach profitability. The converse is also true. If your products and services are greatly underpriced, you will not be as successful as you might be had they been priced appropriately. Pricing, therefore, becomes an issue of great importance. You must not only price your products and services fairly, but you must also price them at a cost that will allow you to compete with other companies making similar offers.

Finally, distribution involves the structures and procedures necessary to bring your products and services to potential customers. If you are unable to distribute your products and services efficiently, sales will suffer.

Together, these four essentials comprise what is known as your *marketing mix*. Each element should complement the others. Different companies will – depending upon the products and services they offer – have different marketing mixes. For some, particularly those that face significant competition, pricing may be the most important factor in their marketing strategy; for others, those that are marketing relatively new products or services, promotion may be the most crucial factor to their success. Your marketing mix should be designed to make your products and services competitive, bringing them to the attention of your customers and showing them in a desirable light and at a fair price.

Following is an example of how marketing mix can be applied to a tour operator in Costa Rica. The product is a five day driving tour that observes the biodiversity of the interior mountains. Promotion would focus on advertising done through appropriate international, regional, and local media. Prices are adjusted according to the season, being higher during peak weeks and reduced during slow periods. Distribution would involve making the tour easily accessible for travelers, perhaps by having the tour start in San Jose, the capital, or at sites frequented by tourists.

The need for an effective marketing plan cannot be underestimated. A carefully developed marketing plan is usually the difference between a successful business and one that fails to attain its promise.

Keys to Effective Advertising

Promotion is built around advertising and all companies promote their products and services. This is what makes advertising so highly competitive.

The average individual in a modern country sees and hears thousands of advertisements each week. From simple classifieds to lavish TV spots that may costs hundreds of thousands of dollars to produce, consumers are bombarded with advertisements. Despite their number and the scope of their subjects, all effective ads share common elements. Understanding these elements can help you to create an advertising campaign that will bring your company to the forefront of your customers' minds.

Following are key points to creating effective advertising:

- Good advertisements always capture the target audience's attention. This may be done through arresting headlines, bold images, catchy situations, or exciting or identifiable scenes. Some ads mix several of these devices, embellishing the ad as necessary to appeal to the audience. TV commercials, for example, take exciting or familiar scenes and add in music and live action. Most ads show people using or needing a product or service.

- After seizing the attention of potential customers, advertisements must arouse interest. This is done most effectively by showing the audience the benefits they can expect to receive by purchasing the product or service.

- Good ads then go on to stimulate desire, showing the target audience why they need to accept what the ad is selling. Desire may be roused through appeals to self-esteem, personal satisfaction, and responsibility.

- Once desire has been stimulated, good advertisements end with a call for action. A call for action may take many forms, but most often includes phrases such as "call or order today," "buy now," "hurry to your local dealer," or "offer valid for a limited time." No matter which phrase is used, a call for action encourages the potential customer to make a commitment to buy the product or service as soon as possible.

To further the impact of advertising, consider the following:

- The message of any ad should be clear and fresh. Consumers have little patience when trying to figure out what an advertisement is selling. If their attention is not captured in the first few seconds, it is unlikely they will pay attention to the rest of the ad.

- Advertisements should be targeted at specific groups. If your products are designed for young adults, advertising in media that are aimed at the forty and up segment will undoubtedly return poor results.

- Use clear, concise, simple language. If people have trouble understanding you, they will not be moved to buy from you.

- Avoid hype and be honest. Do not make promises that you can not keep and which your audience will recognize as being unrealistic or outlandish.

- Create advertisements that are positive. Negative ads, can work, but ads in positive tones generally work better.

- Design advertisements to which your target audience can relate. If, for example, your target audience is the vacationing family, ads depicting fun-filled vacation scenes with which the typical family can identify will have a better chance of being effective than ads that show the family in unusual or challenging scenes in which the vacation theme is relegated to the background.

Promoting your company's products and services through advertising can, without question, increase your sales. Yet, promotion is only one part of an overall market plan, which must also include an analysis of your potential customers, pricing, and distribution.

Your Investment in the Travel and Tourism Industry

Opportunity abounds in travel and tourism. Whereas not long ago only the major cities of the world and a few prime vacation meccas offered entrepreneurs the chance to start new companies, now opportunity may be found around the world.

As travel for business and pleasure becomes more common, companies will emerge to offer a host of products and services, many of them familiar, but many which will be designed to satisfy niche markets. In most cases, these niche markets may be limited in their scope but not in their potential. Many are awaiting to be discovered by entrepreneurs who recognize the opportunities awaiting them.

One of the most innovative ways to explore possible investment sites throughout the world is via your own travel agency. After establishing a travel agency, the entrepreneur/ owner receives numerous benefits enjoyed by travel agents, most notably reduced rates for transportation, accommodations, tours, and cruises. Taking advantage of these benefits enables the entrepreneur to travel at a fraction of the cost of the typical traveler, giving him a vital advantage in seeking worldwide investment opportunities.

About the Author

Over the past 25 years, Adam Starchild has been the author of over two dozen books, and hundreds of magazine articles, primarily on business and finance. His articles have appeared in a wide range of publications around the world -- including Business Credit, Euromoney, Finance, The Financial Planner, International Living, Offshore Financial Review, Reason, Tax Planning International, The Bull & Bear, Trust & Estates, and many more.

Now semi-retired, he was the president of an international consulting group specializing in banking, finance and the development of new businesses, including tourist enterprises. He has owned and operated travel agencies, travel wholesalers, and tour operators.

Although this formidable testimony to expertise in his field, plus his current preoccupation with other books-in-progress, would not seem to leave time for a well-rounded existence, Starchild has won two Presidential Sports Awards and written several cookbooks, and is currently involved in a number of personal charitable projects.

His personal website is at http://www.adamstarchild.com/